Your First
BUDGERIGAR

CW00327960

Photos by:
 Michael Gilroy
 Harry V. Lacey
 Wayne Wallach
 Susan C. Miller
 Robert Pearcy
 Vincent Serbin
 Louise van der Meid

© 1991
By T.F.H.
Publications,
Inc., Neptune,
N.J. 07753 USA
•
T.F.H.
Publications,
The Spinney,
Parklands,
Denmead,
Portsmouth
PO7 6AR
England

Preface

The Budgerigar is one of the best known parrots and the most popular pet bird all over the world. Also popularly known as the Parakeet, the Budgerigar is known taxonomically as *Melopsittacus undulatus*.

Worldwide appreciation for the Budgerigar is due to a number of factors, such as its cheerful disposition, hardy nature, ease of feeding and keeping, etc. Nonetheless, every year millions of Budgerigars suffer from unnecessary disease and inadequate feeding and keeping conditions; they become obese because of insufficient exercise; they get colds and fatal respiratory disease due to chills and drafty environmental conditions; they suffer and die from enteritis due to the lack of clean drinking water. This publication will help you to keep your pet Budgie healthy.

WILD BUDGERIGARS

Wild Budgerigars are nomadic birds that live in large flocks in the semiarid parts of Australia, flying from water hole to water hole. Their diet consists of ripe and half-ripe seeds (particularly millet), green feed and small insects, when available. Wild Budgerigars are somewhat smaller than those bred in captivity.

The Australian spring and early summer (October-December) is the usual breeding time, when an abundance of fresh feed and water is available. Small tree holes are used as nests, sometimes widened and sparsely padded. Brooding is done by the hen. During this time she is fed by the cock, who has no access to the clutch until after hatching.

Temperatures in continental Australia vary a great deal. By nature Budgerigars are quite a hardy species which will tolerate freezing point temperatures, if necessary. Nevertheless, under non-native climatic conditions they cannot survive without our help. Budgerigars kept in outdoor aviaries need insulated draft-free sleeping quarters, where they are protected from extreme cold.

Budgies are the world's most popular bird because they are small and easy to tame and breed.

Structure

The structure and function of birds and mammals are similar, but there are some differences that are important for understanding the keeping, feeding and disease prevention of Budgerigars.

FEATHERS AND SKIN

Avian skin is very thin; it lacks sweat glands and sebaceous glands and is covered by feathers, which are changed through the process of molting. Young Budgerigars first molt at about the age of three months, depending on the season of hatching. Young Budgerigars hatched in autumn may be considerably delayed in molting. Molting usually occurs once a year; it may take several months and is often induced by drastic changes in the environmental temperature. Tail feathers are usually shed in spring and autumn.

RESPIRATORY SYSTEM

Apart from the usual sinuses, trachea, bronchi and lungs (as in mammalian species) birds have air-sacs. These are thin sac-like protrusions from the lungs into the chest and abdominal cavity. They can play an important role during the course of respiratory diseases.

DIGESTIVE SYSTEMS

The avian digestive system consists of an oral cavity, esophagus and crop, proventriculus, gizzard, and a relatively short intestine. Birds do not have teeth. Budgerigars dehull larger seeds before they swallow them. The dehulled seeds are ground in the muscular stomach, which is typical for herbivorous birds. This grinding action is assisted by sand and small stones (grit), which the birds swallow when they have access to them. Sometimes sharp pieces of metal, plastic, glass, etc., are mistaken for grit and swallowed, leading to painful interior injuries from which the bird may die.

REPRODUCTIVE SYSTEM

The reproductive system of female birds consists of ovaries and oviduct. The testicles of male birds are inside the abdominal cavity and cannot be seen or palpated from outside. Male Budgerigars do not have a penis. Copulation is achieved by pressing the male and female cloacas together.

Cuttlebone aids digestion.

Notice the difference in color and feather development. A Budgie's feathers should be smooth, like the Budgie shown here, and not ruffled, like the Budgie shown on the facing page.

Buying

Pet birds are usually purchased from a reputable petshop.
Before you even enter the vendor's premises, have a good look at environmental conditions. The place should be clean, tidy and draft-free.

HEALTHY BIRDS

Judging the health of an animal requires experience and a bit of good luck. Let the vendor do the handling of the bird, even if you are an experienced bird handler yourself. Handling is a severe stress to untamed birds, and birds have been known to die from acute heart failure before or after handling.

Before getting close to the bird, stand back and observe its activity. Healthy birds are alert, hop from perch to perch and show natural shyness. Lack of shyness is often a sign of illness, not of tameness.

The breathing of healthy Budgerigars is quiet, fairly rapid with the beak closed. An open beak and respiratory noises, watery or creamy discharge from the eyes and cere (waxy skin around nasal openings) are signs of a respiratory problem. The beak should close and the bird must be able to dehull seeds.

The plumage should be smooth and shiny, without feathering defects, except during molting. Spiky head feathers and a fluffed plumage (to conserve heat) are signs of illness. The vent feathers should be clean and dry; dirty vent feathers are usually an indication of intestinal or kidney diseases.

The droppings of a normal and healthy Budgerigar are green, harden quickly and have a white "cap," which is the material excreted by the kidneys.

Reject any bird with fluffed up plumage, eye or nose discharge, feather defects, crusty skin, dirty vent, overgrown or open beak, missing toes or labored breathing. Also reject healthy looking birds which have contact with sick ones.

SINGLE BIRD, PAIR OR MIXED GROUP?

If possible, keep a pair or a mixed group rather than a single bird, as it means more enjoyment for both the birds and the owner. Wild Budgerigars in their natural habitat in Australia live in large flocks, and mixing sexes is usually no problem, except occasionally during breeding. However, such birds will spend more time with each other than with the bird keeper and are likely to become less tame than a single bird.

It may be justified to keep a single bird when a close relationship with a lonely, chronically ill or immobile person is to be established. Single birds have no other living contact, so they will need a great deal of human attention and a lot of toys to keep themselves amused and stimulated. Budgerigars left alone for long periods of time may become frustrated and depressed and might start to peck out their own feathers from boredom. This "vice" is very difficult to stop once the bird has discovered that it keeps it amused.

MALE OR FEMALE?

This question is not important in single birds because both sexes make nice pets, but if you want a breeding pair, sexing adult Budgerigars is an important concern. Healthy cocks have a blue or violet cere (waxy skin around nasal openings), hens have a brown cere. Sexing young birds before they are four months of age is largely speculation.

Before their first molt, young Budgerigars are easily recognized. At the age of four weeks they are fully feathered and have dark horizontal stripes between cere and nape.

Telling the age of older birds is much more difficult. Some joints, particularly foot joints, may be swollen due to gout in elderly Budgerigars.

COLOR MUTATIONS

Breeding Budgerigars is a very rewarding field for the enthusiastic aviculturist because Budgerigars abound in color mutations. There are four color series based on two ground colors. The *green* and *yellow* color series are based on a yellow

ground color, the *blue* and *white* color on a white ground color. These four colors occur in light, medium and dark shades, and three additional color factors complicate the picture. The Budgerigar Society recognizes over 100 standard color varieties. Interested readers can refer to books concentrating on breeding Budgerigars.

Some of the common color varieties are the light green, dark green, olive green, sky blue, cobalt, mauve, light yellow, dark yellow, and olive yellow. Other varieties include the red-eyed albinos and lutinos, the bicolored pied Budgerigars (Variegateds, Harlequins), opalines (with a V-shaped color area between the wings), cinnamons (greywings, lacewings, recessive pieds, crested Budgerigars, etc.).

These color mutants may appear attractive, but their character is no different from that of standard ground color Budgies. So there is no need to be choosy about color if you just want a cheerful pet bird.

Budgies come in many colors and body shapes.

Behavior

For transport of your Budgie, use either a transport box with holes or wire netting on only one side or a small transport cage covered by a cloth, which should prevent drafts. An untamed Budgie should not be transported in a large cage as it might panic and hurt itself.

QUARANTINE

Bird keepers who already own other birds are well advised to keep any newcoming bird separate and under observation (quarantined), until they can be reasonably sure that it is healthy. Sick birds, no matter what disease was diagnosed, must never be allowed to join healthy ones. But even with quarantined birds there can be no absolute guarantee that the bird is not a disease carrier who simply shows no symptoms.

Apart from the risk of transmissible diseases, new birds may have problems adjusting to their new environment. They may be bullied by other birds or may turn out to be rowdies themselves. It may be helpful to place the newcomer in a small cage (e.g., transport or show cage) within the aviary for just a few days until it is accepted by the bird community.

MIXING WITH OTHER AVIAN SPECIES

In Australia wild Budgerigars live in large flocks, so that living together with many conspecifics is part of their natural behavior. They are normally quite peaceful birds, but there may arise arguments about partners and favorite nesting spots. Budgerigars mix well with many other small parrots like Cockatiels but they may bully Canaries.

MIXING WITH OTHER PETS

Budgerigars may be kept with trained docile dogs but not with cats. However, at the beginning, dogs and Budgies should not be left alone. If you have a cat in the house, your Budgerigar should be permanently caged in a large flight cage, and the cat should have no access to the room with the cage.

Keep your Budgie away from cats.

The Budgie's cage should be sturdy, with heavy wire grilling, to protect it from the claws of cats.

Cages

The minimum cage size for a single Budgie should be 24 inches (60 cm.) long, 20 inches (50 cm.) high, and 16 inches (40 cm.) deep, so that the bird can spread its wings without touching the cage wire. The cage for a pair should be longer, at least 28 inches (70 cm.) long. Many Budgie cages do not reach these postulated dimensions, which is unfortunate because undersized cages restrict the bird's exercise and are a common cause of obesity.

At least two sides of the cage wire should be arranged horizontally for climbing, and the spacing of the wire should be narrow enough to prevent birds from getting their head stuck between the wire. Some breeders and veterinarians dislike round cages because they are said to confuse the bird's orientation. Round cages also tend to be too small to permit sufficient exercise.

Your pet dealer will be able to show you a selection of cages and explain the differences between the various designs and materials so that you can see which is best for your use.

SAND, GRIT, GRILL

Budgies like to spend some of their time on the ground where they search for grit, small stones and sand that help the muscular stomach (gizzard) grind the dehulled seeds. Do not use metal grills as they prevent the bird's access to the bottom of the cage. These grills are intended to keep the birds separated from their own droppings, but their disadvantages outweigh their advantages. If the recommended cleaning routine is followed, the risk of catching a disease from the droppings on the bottom of the cage is quite minimal.

Gravel paper, i.e., paper with sand or seeds glued onto it, may assist in keeping the bird's toe nails trimmed but it does not satisfy the desire to pick and scratch in the sand on the floor. Also, gravel paper does not soften the impact of the bird's landing on the floor, which might be considerable because the bird cannot make full use of its wings inside the narrow cage. This could result in lameness due to injuries to the foot pad, joints, ligaments and tendons.

PERCHES

Cages available in petshops have wooden or plastic perches with a standard diameter. It is beneficial to replace these perches with natural branches that have varying diameters, predominantly between 0.5–2.0 cm. This forces the bird to constantly alter its toe muscles when hopping from perch to perch. The branches can be from various deciduous trees (fruit, maple, elm, willow, beech, larch, etc.) and shrubs, and should be free of droppings from wild birds. It is advisable to wash the branches before placing them in the cage.

Apart from the toe exercise, natural branches have other benefits. Budgerigars chew the rind, which contains vitamins and other nutrients, which also keeps them amused. Once the natural branches are chewed clean (normally after 1-3 months), they should be replaced with new ones.

Perches should not obstruct the narrow space within the cage. If two perches are at least 16 inches (40 cm.) apart and there is no obstacle between them, the Budgerigar will have to use its wings to jump from perch to perch. Leave a distance of 4 inches (10 cm.) between perch and wire so that tail feathers do not rub against the wire during turning. To prevent the contamination of feed or water containers with droppings, perches should not be fitted above them.

CAGE FITTINGS

Other cage fittings include drinkers, feed containers, waterbowls, cuttlefish bones and toys. Toys are important for single Budgerigars that are often alone, but toys that severely obstruct the inner space of the cage should be removed.

A common type of drinker consists of a plastic bottle with a metal spout for drinking. The bottle clips to the cage side and the system relies on gravity. The spout must be of durable material to resist the Budgie's chewing forces and should be cleaned regularly to remove algae, which tend to grow on the inside of the drinker. Other types of water containers are open cups made of heavy plastic, earthenware or porcelain. Drinking water is best not put on the floor where it might be soiled by droppings.

The drinking water should be changed at least twice daily because a number of bacteria (e.g., coli, staphylococci, etc.) may multiply rapidly, particularly under warm conditions. Contaminated water can lead to severe and often lethal crop and gut infections and some birds might refuse to drink altogether.

Most Budgerigars like to have a bath at least every other day, although there are some that seem to dislike water. Baths are either transparent bath houses (a dark bath might scare the bird) or shallow tip-proof saucers placed on the floor. A little sand at the bottom of the bath prevents slipping. The water must be tepid and must be changed daily. Bath saucers should be removed after the daily bath to prevent further wetting of the cage. Antiparasitic bath additives should only be used if ectoparasites were actually diagnosed because many birds drink from the water in which they bathe.

Feeders should be made of durable material (earthenware, porcelain, heavy plastic) to prevent destruction of the container and ingestion of fragments by the bird. Usually the feeders are fitted on the inside of the cage. Feed containers on the floor are easily soiled by droppings.

Budgerigars dehull the seeds before swallowing the kernel, leaving a lot of empty hulls lying around. The empty hulls should be blown from the top of the seed containers to make sure that there is sufficient feed left. Fresh or green feed, sprouted feed, fruit and vegetables should be offered in a separate container or may be clipped to the cage wire.

Cuttlefish bone belongs in every cage. It is usually clipped to the cage wire. The bird uses it for beak trimming and as a source of calcium and phosphorous.

A variety of toys are available for the amusement of birds (and bird keepers). They include entire playgrounds, swings, bells, balls, mirrors, ladders, etc. As long as they do not restrict the bird's movements and consist of unbreakable material, they serve a useful purpose, particularly for single, lonely birds. But do not overload the interior of the cage with them.

Nestboxes are a prerequisite for successful breeding. According to some experts, their minimum dimensions should be 5.5 x 6 inches (13 x 15 cm.) at the base and 16 inches (20 cm.) high. The entrance hole should be off center and should be approximately 1.8 inches (4.5 cm.) wide. At the bottom of the cage there should be a shallow depression for the eggs. It should also be somewhat off center but to the other side of the entrance hole. There is usually a perch outside the entrance hole and a lid that serves

The cage should be equipped with exercise toys.

This cage has horizontal grilling which enables the Budgie to exercise by climbing up and down the cage. But be VERY CAREFUL where you locate the cage. Placing it next to a pot on the stove could result in the Budgie being asphyxiated or over-heated. The cage should be hung from a cage stand at about the height of the person's face who will be its trainer.

as an inspection flap. The outside of the nestbox should have a rough surface to facilitate the climbing of the young Budgerigars.

Nestbox hygiene is key to the survival and future development of the nestlings. Nestboxes should be disposable or easy to clean. Disposable boxes made of cardboard have definite hygienic advantages but are cumbersome to make. Nondisposable nestboxes, made of chipwood, solid timber or plywood should be cleaned and disinfected before each new clutch. Brooding temperatures and humidity inside the nestbox favor the growth of fungi, which can cause fatal respiratory infections. Large crevices, cracks, extra ventilation holes and open inspection flaps may be responsible for drafts and chilling of the nestlings. Nesting material should consist of highly absorbent sawdust or fine woodshavings.

LOCATION

The location of the cage can be very important for the bird's physical and mental health. The bird, particularly—but not only—the single bird, needs contact with the family. Therefore, the cage should be at approximately the same height as a human head (because this is the part of a human that a Budgerigar is most familiar with) and should be in a light, draft-free location. The bird must also have an opportunity to retreat from the direct sunlight.

The kitchen is too damp and too dangerous for flying exercise, halls are too drafty, and bedrooms usually too quiet. Also, the bird should not be carried around from room to room. So, the most logical place for a cage is often the family room, where the TV set is located in many households. TV light neither harms nor spoils your Budgerigar, but the bird should be several meters away from the set and outside the direct line between remote control and television.

LIGHTING/TEMPERATURE

It was already mentioned above that the cage should be located in a well-lighted spot that also offers shade. The normal light in a family home is sufficient.

In locations where sudden noises at night must be taken into account, it is good practice not to switch out the light altogether but to leave on a dim light so that if the bird becomes alarmed it will not flutter around aimlessly in the dark. Covering the cage at night with a cloth that lets fresh air in is useful under moderate climatic conditions; however, this practice may be dangerous when it is hot.

Budgerigars are relatively hardy birds. Under their native conditions in Australia they sometimes even experience light frosts. Nevertheless, extreme temperature fluctuations should be avoided and excessive heat often does more harm than good. Temperatures between 62 to 74°F (17 to 24°C), depending on the relative humidity, should be comfortable for Budgerigars.

Exercise

Many cages are too small to allow a Budgerigar sufficient flying exercise, particularly cages overloaded with all sorts of toys, ladders, etc. Therefore Budgerigars should be allowed regular flying exercise in a room.

Flying exercise is associated with a number of risks for both bird and homeowner. Before allowing a new bird out of the cage for flying exercise you should be sure that the bird is sufficiently tame and that all danger spots have been removed. Other pets, particularly cats, dogs and larger parrots should be out of the room. In order to avoid collision between your bird and windowpanes, glass doors, mirrors and the like, they should be screened or the curtains drawn. Other common danger spots are open vessels containing fluids (e.g., open jugs with milk or juice) vases, open aquariums, lit fireplaces, heaters, stoves, candles, spiny plants and objects, open gaps and drawers. Kitchen, bathrooms, laundry room, workshops, garage, attic, laboratory, etc., are therefore totally unsuitable locations for your bird's flying exercise. Also, there should be no access to drugs, tobacco, coffee, alcohol, chemicals, cosmetics, ink, lead, or toxic plants.

Larger parrots are notorious for their destructive behavior and the damage they can do to electric cables, wall papers, lamp shades, pictures, etc. This problem is less pronounced with the relatively small Budgerigar.

Budgerigars will spend most of their time on certain perches. The area underneath such perches should be protected so that droppings are easily removed and the uric acid does not damage the furniture or carpets.

The bird should never be fed outside the cage. If it knows that feed is only available inside the cage, it will usually return to the cage in due time without the necessity of chasing and catching it. The cage door should always be open and there should be a perch in front of it to facilitate getting inside. If the bird has to be caught, use a cloth or a fine mesh, not the naked hand. Tame birds will perch on a finger and are thus easily carried into the cage.

If you cannot allow your Budgie out of the cage to fly around, give him exercise toys. Special Budgie balls are available and are just one of many toys made especially for Budgies.

Aviary

Your budgerigars can be kept in outdoor aviaries, as long as certain conditions are met. Principally, outdoor aviaries should be draft-free and dry; they should face the sun and include a shaded, insulated shelter room. Proximity to industrial smoke, busy and noisy traffic, pigeon lofts, other aviaries and poultry plants is best avoided. Vermin and moist conditions are prevented by a sloping concrete floor and narrow guage wire mesh. For cost reasons this type of construction is often rejected out of hand. An alternative is a floor consisting of fine and rough gravel covered by dry sand. Such an alternative may sound attractive to people with access to plenty of clean sand (e.g., beaches, quarries, river beds). Vermin can be kept out by a fine wire mesh at the bottom of the aviary.

Outdoor aviaries are usually constructed of iron or wooden stakes and narrow gauge wire, consisting preferably of two joggled layers. The two layers should stop vermin, cat paws, wild birds, etc., from getting in and prevent small birds from getting their head stuck. Freshly galvanized wire may lead to zinc poisoning, if chewed by birds. Plastic coating on wire mesh is likely to be chewed off. Cracks and crevices in wooden stakes offer red mites an excellent hiding and breeding environment. Painting with nontoxic paint at regular intervals should destroy such breeding grounds.

Outdoor aviaries should be partly or fully covered by a roof, so that droppings from wild birds, which might contain pathogenic bacteria or

Keeping your Budgies in an outside aviary can be very rewarding, especially if you ae interested in mass breeding. Be sure you use very small, heavy mesh screening to keep out predators. Keep a large bird net handy to capture birds easily without injuring them. Bring a normal cage into the aviary (see photo facing) to hold the birds you have netted.

parasites, are kept out. Feed and water containers should always be placed in the covered section. Under cold climatic conditions freezing of drinking water may be a problem. Change water frequently, use containers with heating elements or place drinkers in the shelter room.

INDOOR AVIARIES

Indoor aviaries are regarded as large cages with sufficient space for exercise. They should be in a light, draft-free location. A dim light should be switched on during the night and artificial ultraviolet light is normally quite superfluous.

ANTICS

The skills of Budgerigars, if allowed to develop to their full potential, are similar to those of Cockatiels. They are excellent and enduring fliers; they love aerobatics, and they can mimic simple words and tunes, although not nearly to the same perfection as some of the larger parrots and mynahs. Young male birds are reputed to be more talented for speech than females. The bird must be very young (from five to six weeks onwards). Start with simple words (e.g., its own name, "hello," etc.). Do not proceed until the first words are repeated correctly. With patient training your Budgie will even learn simple tricks, such as lying on its back, spreading its wings, pulling a wagon, etc.

TAMING

Budgerigars are relatively easy to tame while still young and kept singly. Taming pairs and older birds is more difficult. Patience is one of the prerequisites for success.

Some authors recommend wing-clipping before taming, although this is not an indispensable prerequisite. Wing-clipping just makes taming easier.

Budgies love to play, so give them lots of toys.

Handling

Some examinations and procedures require the bird to be held firmly. It should be taken into the hand regularly, to which the healthy bird should not take offense, as long as it can breathe freely. However, with obese birds the situation is different. Obese birds not used to being handled regularly may die of sudden heart failure due to stress.

Unlike larger parrots or cockatiels, Budgerigars can nip but not bite you. Nevertheless, you may wish to put on a light glove. Heavy-duty gloves should not be used because you may have problems controlling your pressure on the bird. When trying to handle a Budgie, the windows should be closed, curtains drawn, lights dimmed but not switched off. Use a fine mesh bird net to catch the bird. Try to talk to the bird in a quiet, calming voice and refrain from hectic movements.

The best way of holding a Budgerigar is to close the palm of your hand over the bird's back and wings, while holding the head tightly between your thumb, index and middle fingers.

There is no unique way to hold a Budgie. This Budgie is being held in order to have its foot wrapped so a broken leg could be mended. It is a good way to hold the Budgie since it's head can be restrained.

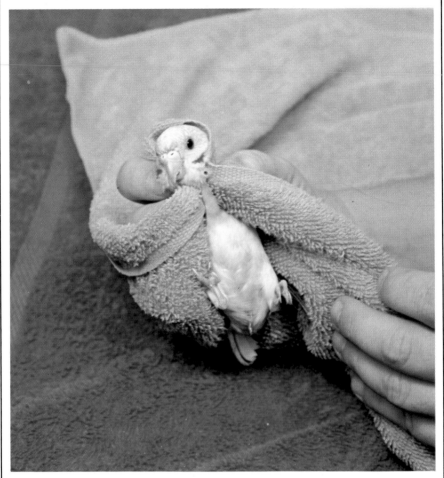

If you are inexperienced or unsure about how to hold a Budgie, throw a light towel over the bird and grip the bird gently through the cloth. Another way to hold the Budgie safely, is to let it perch on a stick (see facing page) and you then can move the bird on the stick.

Cleaning

Cage

and cage furnishings must be kept clean, particularly in cages and aviaries with a large number of birds, where the disease risk is greater than in cages with only one or two birds. Hygienic conditions can reduce but not eliminate the risk of infectious disease. Infectious agents can reach their hosts via the feed, water, air, or by contact. Vermin, such as rats, mice, flies, cockroaches, and wild birds may be disease carriers without showing signs of illness themselves. Unhygienic conditions acting as a severe stress can even predispose birds to noninfectious diseases.

CLEANLINESS, TIDINESS

Without cleanliness, tidiness, clean air and smooth water-repellent surfaces, hygiene is impossible. Modern cages made of wire and plastic are obviously easier to clean than bamboo or wooden cages. Tidying and cleaning up before disinfection is by far more important than the disinfection itself because disinfectants cannot fulfill their function if the disease agents to be killed are protected by dirt and organic matter.

STEPS TO HYGIENIC CONDITIONS

Cleaning and disinfection is done in several successive steps:

1. Tidying up and removing grossly visible dirt, using vacuum cleaner, shovel, scraper, wire brush, etc.

2. Soaking in water (containing detergent or other mild cleaning agent) for up to one day.

3. Cleaning with hard brush, scraper, wire brush, water, including the use of steam cleaning equipment in outdoor aviaries. Steam cleans well but does not sterilize under these conditions because it cools too fast.

4. Drying. Without drying, the water left from the previous steps would dilute the concentration of the disinfectants to be employed in the following step.

5. Disinfection with one of the many disinfectants available in petshops.

DISINFECTANTS

Many cleaning agents and disinfectants are available from drug stores, chemist shops, petshops. They are effective against common bacteria, viruses and fungi, but rarely against parasite eggs.

Prevention of ectoparasites requires an understanding of the biology of these parasites. The single most important ectoparasites of Budgerigars are knemidokoptic mites (scaly face or scaly leg mites). They live permanently in or on the skin of their hosts and require a special therapeutic approach. Treatment for other mites involves spraying of aviary and birds with insecticides, which must be handled with caution because they are highly toxic to man and bird alike.

CLEANING ROUTINE

Daily. Change feed, remove perishable fruit and vegetables. Change drinking water at least twice daily, after cleaning the water containers. Change bathing water and clean bath. Check nestboxes of breeders if birds are not disturbed. Remove droppings, large particles and wet patches from the sand.

Weekly. Tidy up and clean aviary and furnishings with water and brush. Renew or sift sand, maybe even twice per week.

Monthly. Clean and disinfect feed and water troughs.

Quarterly-to-semiannually. Change natural perches, renew superficial sand layer.

If your pet Budgie sits hunched and puffed up on its perch, you can be sure something is wrong. Oftentimes the problem is due to the drinking water being soiled or the food being spoiled. Parasites can also cause distress in birds. Consult your petshop or veterinarian if your bird isn't acting right.

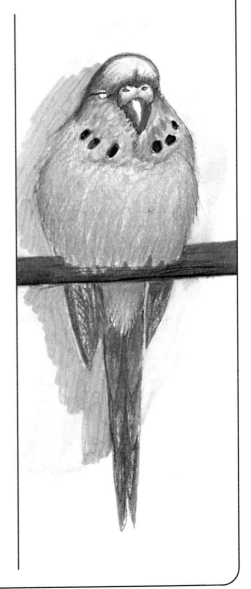

In order to maintain a healthy Budgie you must have a routine. This cleaning routine is described in detail on page 25. It is of the utmost importance that the cage you buy for your Budgie can easily be cleaned. It should have a bottom that pulls out so you can remove the droppings, change the seed, etc. When visiting your petshop (facing page) to select a cage, keep this in mind.

Nutrition

Life without water can't exist on earth. Water is the single most important part of the diet. It is a grave error to believe that Budgerigars as natural inhabitants of semiarid zones do not depend on good quality water.

Drinking water should be clean, free of chlorine and other disinfectants and chemical additives. Strongly chlorinated tap water is best left standing for a few hours in a bowl with a large surface to permit the chlorine gas to escape. Boiling the water kills germs but makes water rather untasty. Water of very poor quality or with a high salt content should not be used. Nongaseous, bottled mineral water is an expensive but safe alternative.

The drinking water should be changed twice daily to prevent the buildup of pathogenic bacteria, mainly coli bacteria, in the drinking water. Coli bacteria can lead to fatal crop and intestinal tract infections, one of the most common causes of vomiting and diarrhea in psittacine birds. Detergents should be used sparingly.

Budgerigars need mixed seeds as a basic diet. Petshops usually have the basic seeds or seed mixtures for sale. These mixtures contain predominantly canary seed, millet, linseed, niger, rape, sometimes oat, wheat or an artificial grain. Artificial grain may consist of flour, dried egg yolk, dried milk, alfalfa meal, iodine, vitamins, etc. Budgerigars also welcome the addition of sunflower seeds and a selection of seeding grasses, which can be dried during the seeding season. Seed mixtures are usually iodized to prevent goiter, a swelling of the thyroid glands due to iodine deficiency. Spray millet is a real treat but should not be given every day because it is very rich in energy.

The above mentioned basic seed diet should be supplemented by a variety of fruit (apple, berries, kiwis, citrus, banana, mango, etc.) and greenfood (chickweed, dandelion, carrots, different types of lettuces, spinach, etc.). Heavily fertilized or insecticide-treated types of lettuce, such as the soft garden lettuce, can lead to indigestion. Firmer types of lettuce (e.g., endive, chicory) are usually much preferred by the birds. Cabbage leaves are not digestible by Budgerigars and must not be given.

Sprouted seeds can *partially* replace greenfood, particularly in winter time, when the type of recommended greenfood may not be readily available. Breeders like feeding sprouted seeds to their breeding birds because they are rich in vitamins and other nutrients. Their preparation is quite simple: soak enough seeds from your usual seed mixture in water to make a day's supply; keep in a warm place for 24 hours; rinse thoroughly several times and leave standing in a warm place for another 24 to 48 hours. Good fresh seeds should have sprouted by then.

Thorough rinsing is important to wash off microscopic fungi that tend to multiply under such conditions. Discard moldy sprouts as they may cause enteritis.

During the brooding and rearing period breeders like to offer various breeding mixtures, soaked wheat bread, boiled eggs, shrimps, cottage cheese, tidbits, etc. However, this kind of feed is perishable and should not be left for more than a few hours, depending both on the food and the environmental conditions.

Breeders will know that chicks are at first fed "crop milk," a protein-rich secretion regurgitated by the feeding hen.

Vitamin preparations are often administered during brooding and rearing. If given in moderate amounts, there are no scientific objections, although a well-balanced diet as described above should suffice.

The daily requirement of vitamins is not easily pinpointed and an overdose could be harmful. However, vitamins may be indicated for brief periods during molting and other stress situations.

Petshops usually offer a variety of stimulating medicines, based on some well-known animal and plant extracts, for the stimulation of the body reserves. They may be useful if given under certain stress situations, but given regularly their effect is usually disappointing.

Birds do not have teeth. Budgerigars dehull the seeds before they swallow them. Further grinding takes place in the strong muscular stomach (gizzard). This grinding action is supported by grit, i.e., stones, grains of sand, grated shells, etc., which must be supplied, and which the birds swallow. Grit is also a source of minerals for the bird.

Junk food, strongly salted or spiced food, cheese, butter, crackers, chips, biscuits, soft drinks and alcohol must not be given to Budgerigars, as much as they might beg for it.

FEEDING TECHNIQUE

Feed and water must be protected from fecal contamination. Most commercial feed containers are protected against such contamination by a hood. For the same reasons, feed containers should be clipped to the cage wire and should not be placed on the floor, unless you have fledglings. They may have trouble finding the feed container, and placing a seed bowl on the floor may help them. Perches must not be fitted directly above feed or water containers.

Check feed containers daily, blow away empty husks from the top of the feed containers, change feed daily and remove perishable fruit and greenfood.

Budgies constantly peck at their feedstuffs. Basically they are seed eaters, but they also will eat green vegetation. Fresh millet sprays are a natural food. Attach it to the cage as shown above. A healthy bird (facing page), *looks* healthy. This young bird (you can tell its young because the stripes on the forehead have not disappeared yet) is the picture of health.

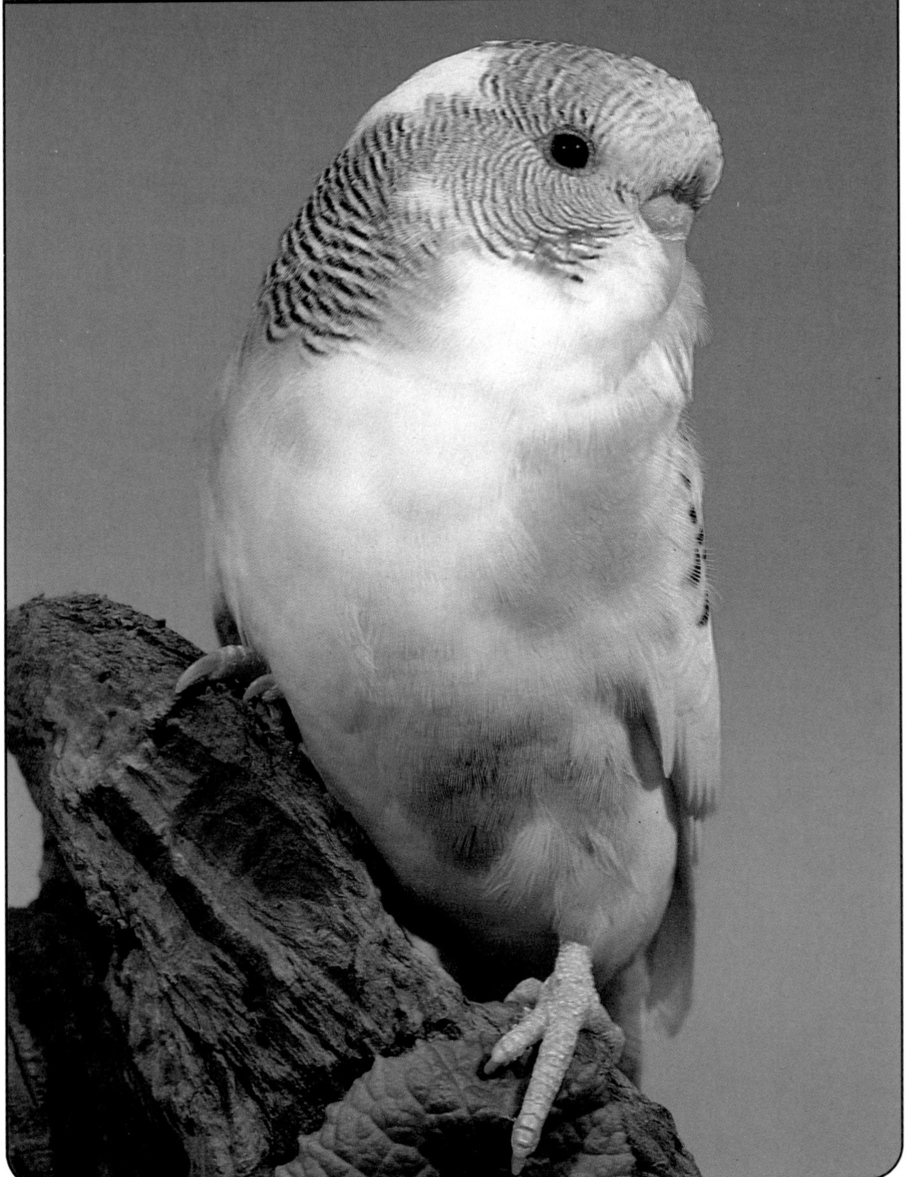

FEED STORAGE

Feed is perishable by nature. Mechanisms involved are fermentation, fungi, bacteria, parasites. Light, high temperature and humidity, lack of ventilation and other factors have an accelerating effect on feed spoilage. As is known to all of us, spoiled food can cause violent diarrhea, vomiting, etc. In birds this is not much different. Moldy feed will lead to diarrhea, liver damage, even vitamin deficiencies and death. Feed spoilage can be slowed down by observing the following storage conditions.

Cool. 50 to 54°F (10–12°C), but not refrigerated, thus reducing condensation.

Dry. Below 70% relative humidity or well ventilated in the tropics. Tightly closed containers are not advisable.

Dark. To reduce the detrimental effect of light on vitamins and fats.

Vermin-proof. Keep out rodents, beetles, mites, flies etc., which use up the feed and might carry disease agents.

Short. Do not buy in bulk unless you have excellent storage facilities.

The aforementioned storage conditions apply to the storage of seeds. Supplemental feed, such as sprouted feed, fruit, greenfeed, cottage cheese, boiled eggs, etc., must be given fresh and removed at the end of the day, if not earlier.

First Aid

Sick Budgerigars lose weight rapidly and must be treated without delay. Haphazard treatment by the owner usually wastes valuable time. Marked changes in the activity level of your Budgie often indicate the onset of sickness. Check with your pet dealer or seek an appointment with a specialized veterinarian as quickly as you can.

Sick birds are often in a state of shock. Offer your Budgie glucose water; feed it but handle it as little as possible. Otherwise it might die in your or the veterinarian's hand.

For transport use a small, warm box with air holes. Do not use a large cage for transport as the frightened bird might flutter around and get hurt, but do take the bird cage along to the vet so he can evaluate keeping and feeding conditions.

Open wounds may be covered by gauze or tissue paper, but do not treat open wounds with iodine or other antiseptics unless advised by the veterinarian. Talk to the bird in a calming voice whenever you see or handle it.

Sick birds should be kept warm, possibly close to infrared light. The bird must be able to retreat if it feels too hot. Heated cages, "hospital cages," are commercially available. Pad the bottom of the cage for very sick birds, supply water and feed and fit a low perch.

Bibliography

ENCYCLOPEDIA OF BUDGERIGARS
By Georg Radtke
ISBN 0-86622-734-2
TFH H-1027
Contents: Care and Breeding. Disease Prevention and Treatment. Care and Training of House Pets. Selective Breeding. The British Show Budgerigars. Color Varieties—Their Origin and Development.
Audience: This book has been written for the many, many thousands of owners of budgerigars who have been captivated by their birds to the point that they want a good body of truly detailed and highly authoritative information. This book provides exactly what they're looking for.
Hard cover, 5½ x 8"; 320 pages
148 full-color photos, 44 B/W photos

BEGINNING WITH BUDGIES
By Anne Ray Streeter
ISBN 0-86622-709-1
TFH PS-839
Contents: Why a Budgerigar? What is a Budgerigar? The Budgerigar as a Pet. Buying a Budgerigar. Taking Your Bird Home. Caring for the Bird. Keeping Your Bird Healthy. Making Friends. Caring for the Sick or Injured Bird. Breeding.
Audience: This excellent book concentrates on discussing in detail the basics of selecting and caring for a budgie. It covers its topic well, providing needed information about how to choose the best bird right through how to sex and breed budgies.
Flexi-cover 5½ x 8", 128 pages.
74 full-color photos, 10B/W photos.

BUDGERIGAR HANDBOOK
By Ernest H. Hart
ISBN 0-86622-134-4
TFH H-901
Contents: Forming A Stud. Modes Of Inheritance. Basic Breeding Techniques. The Mechanics Of Breeding. Aviaries And Equipment. Feeding And Management. Selection And Upgrading. Trouble Hints And Ailments. Shows And The Standard. Matings And Color Expectation. Training The Pet Budgerigar. The Future.
Hard cover, 5½ x 8½", 251 pages
67 black and white photos, 104
 color photos

**A Step-By-Step Book About
Budgerigars/Parakeets**
By Georg A. Radtke
Softcover Sk-002: ISBN 0-86622-463-7
Lib. B. SK-002X: ISBN 0-86622-912-4
Over 50 full-color photos and drawings;
5½ x 8½", 64 pages.

THE JOY OF BUDGERIGARS
By Howard Richmond
ISBN 0-86622-082-8
TFH PS-799
Contents: Budgies as Pets. Cages and Accessories. Choosing Your Budgie. Feeding Your Budgie. Health Care. Emergencies. Some Thoughts About Taming and Training. Taming Your Budgie. Teaching Your Budgie Tricks. Teaching Your Budgie to Talk.
Hard cover, 5½ x 8", 96 pages.
Contains 48 full-color photos, over 20
 black and white photos.

THESE BOOKS ARE AVAILABLE AT YOUR LOCAL PETSHOP.